The Settling of
Jamestown

MaryLee Knowlton and Janet Riehecky

Gareth Stevens Publishing
A WORLD ALMANAC EDUCATION GROUP COMPANY

Please visit our web site at: www.garethstevens.com
For a free color catalog describing Gareth Stevens Publishing's list of high-quality books and multimedia programs, call 1-800-542-2595 (USA) or 1-800-387-3178 (Canada). Gareth Stevens Publishing's fax: (414) 332-3567.

Library of Congress Cataloging-in-Publication Data

Knowlton, MaryLee.
    The settling of Jamestown / by MaryLee Knowlton and Janet Riehecky.
      p. cm. — (Events that shaped America)
    Summary: A description of the struggles of the English settlers in the colony of Jamestown, from 1607 to 1698, and their relationship with the neighboring Algonquian Indians.
    Includes bibliographical references and index.
    ISBN 0-8368-3225-6 (lib. bdg.)
    1. Jamestown (Va.)—History—17th century—Juvenile literature. 2. Frontier and pioneer life—Virginia—Jamestown—Juvenile literature. 3. Virginia—History—Colonial period, ca. 1600-1775—Juvenile literature. [1. Jamestown (Va.)—History—17th century.
2. Virginia—History—Colonial period, ca. 1600-1775.] I. Riehecky, Janet, 1953- II. Title.
III. Series.
F234.J3K65   2002
75.5'425101—dc21   2002021053

This North American edition first published in 2002 by
Gareth Stevens Publishing
A World Almanac Education Group Company
330 West Olive Street, Suite 100
Milwaukee, WI 53212 USA

This edition © 2002 by Gareth Stevens Publishing.

Produced by Discovery Books
Editor: Sabrina Crewe
Designer and page production: Sabine Beaupré
Photo researcher: Sabrina Crewe
Maps and diagrams: Stefan Chabluk
Gareth Stevens editorial direction: Mark J. Sachner
Gareth Stevens art direction: Tammy Gruenewald
Gareth Stevens production: Susan Ashley

Photo credits: Association for the Preservation of Virginia Antiquities, pp. 16, 27 (bottom); Corbis, pp. 4, 6; Granger Collection, pp. 9, 20, 24; Jamestown-Yorktown Foundation, pp. 11, 26, 27 (top); National Park Service, Colonial National Historical Park, cover, pp. 12, 14, 17, 18; North Wind Picture Archives, pp. 7, 8, 10, 13, 19, 21, 22, 23, 25.

Printed in the United States of America

1 2 3 4 5 6 7 8 9 06 05 04 03 02

Contents

Introduction 4

Chapter 1: Virginia People 6

Chapter 2: The Trip from England 10

Chapter 3: The Struggle to Survive 12

Chapter 4: Life in Virginia 20

Chapter 5: The End of Jamestown 24

Conclusion 26

Time Line 28

Things to Think About and Do 29

Glossary 30

Further Information 31

Index 32

Introduction

The Old World Meets the New World

In the spring of 1607, three ships landed on a **swampy** coast in North America. Aboard were 139 men and 4 boys who had come from England.

The travelers landed in what we know today as the state of Virginia. There, they built a small village that they named Jamestown. This would become the first English **colony** in what the settlers called "the **New World**." But they were not the first people there. The land was already home to the Algonquians, Native people who lived in hundreds of small villages throughout the area.

This book tells the story of these two groups of people. It tells who they were and how they helped each other. It also tells how they hurt each other and how it all turned out.

A pair of Algonquian chiefs in Virginia in the late 1500s.

What the Colonists Wrote

Several of the Jamestown colonists kept journals. Others wrote letters to relatives and to newspapers. These are our written records of what happened at Jamestown, but they are not always the truth. Some of their accounts were attempts to persuade more settlers to come to the new colony. In those accounts they left out the illnesses, hunger, and dangers of their new life. Instead they wrote of the beauty and bounty of the land and of their own heroic actions.

Who Were the Newcomers?

About half of the new colonists were "gentlemen." They came from rich families who had servants to do their work and take care of them. These were some of the others: a pastor, a tailor, two doctors, a blacksmith, two bricklayers, one mason, four carpenters, and a few soldiers. Sadly, it would turn out, there were no farmers.

The remaining colonists were poor people who had agreed to work for seven years as servants to pay for the cost of their trip to the New World. For those seven years they were called **indentured servants**, but they were treated as slaves.

Why Had They Come?

The New World held bright promise for people from England. The rich men hoped to find gold and then go back. Some of the others hoped to start a new life in a new land and for a chance to make their fortunes.

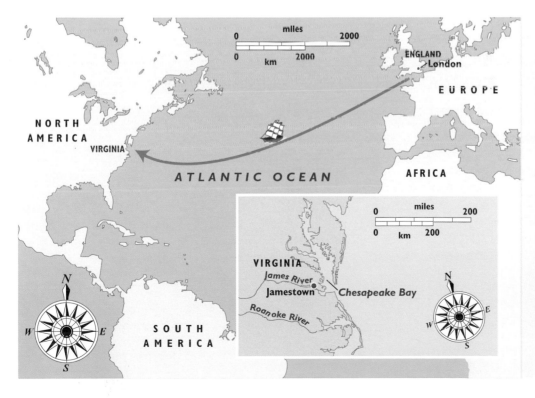

This map shows the route taken by the three ships carrying the colonists from England to Virginia. The small map shows the region of Virginia where they founded their settlement.

Chapter One

Virginia People

This Algonquian village was **fortified** by a wooden fence.

Before the Englishmen arrived, the land along the Atlantic coast was already home to the Algonquian people. They lived in villages scattered throughout the area. Many of the villages had their own particular traditions and languages.

Village Life

The villages were usually built near a river or lake. Some were small, but others had several hundred houses. Villagers built a wall of wooden posts around the village for protection.

Between six and twenty people lived in each house. Children often lived with their grandparents, uncles, aunts, and cousins as well as their parents. The houses had wooden frames that were built by the men, who were the woodworkers in the villages. The frames were covered by mats that women made from plant fibers and animal skins. The frames could stand against the harsh winds and the mats were so tightly woven that no wind or rain could get through.

Dividing the Work

The jobs of men and women were clearly separated. Men were the hunters and worked in stone, metal, and wood. They were also the warriors and usually the leaders of the group.

The women did textile work. They wove nets for trapping animals and baskets for storage. Besides the tight mats that formed walls of the houses, they wove looser mats for drying corn and other foods that needed to be kept for the winter or for traveling.

Hunters and Farmers

The Algonquians, like other Native peoples, lived according to the natural world that provided their food. The men were expert hunters and fishermen. They used many parts of the animal: meat for food, bones for tools, and skins and fur for clothes and warmth.

The women were the farmers in the community. Their main crop was corn, but they also raised pumpkins, beans, and melons.

The Virginia groups fished with traps, spears, and nets. The waters in the area provided plenty of fish.

Decoration

"In each eare commonly they have three great holes, whereat they hange chaines, bracelets, or copper. Some of their men weare in those holes, a smal greene and yellow coloured snake, neare halfe a yard [0.5 meter] in length, which crawling and lapping her selfe about his necke often times familiarly would kiss his lips. Others wear a dead Rat tied by the tail."

Jamestown colonist John Smith writing about the Algonquian people he met

Corn, or maize, as the settlers called it, was a useful food for the Indians. It was delicious and nutritious when fresh and a lifesaver when dried. Corn could be used in many ways when there was no fresh food available. It could be carried in a pouch by travelers or ground into meal for making bread. In the winter, Native people and white settlers combined corn with water and cooked a cereal to nourish themselves until spring came again. The strong fibers of the husks and corn silk made good mats and baskets.

This picture shows an Algonquian village with crops, such as corn and pumpkins, at different stages of the growth and harvest cycle.

The Powhatan

The most powerful group of Algonquians in Virginia in 1607 was the Powhatan. Their leader was Wahunsonacock, who changed his name to Powhatan when he took over from his father. He ruled over the six groups his father had organized into the Powhatan **Confederacy** as well as twenty more that he had conquered. Each group had its own chief. At the time that the Jamestown settlers arrived, Powhatan ruled a nation of more than ten thousand people living in two hundred villages.

When the Englishmen arrived on their three ships, they claimed for themselves the land of the Powhatan. At first, the Native people of Virginia thought the new people were interesting—if a little strange—and possibly useful. The English felt the same way about the Indians. It would not be long before the two cultures learned to take each other very seriously as both friend and enemy.

Men and Women
"The men [spend] their times in fishing, hunting, wars, and such manlike exercises. . . . The women and children make mats, baskets, pots, morters, pound their corne, make their bread, prepare their victuals, plant their corne, gather their corne, beare al kind of burdens, and such like."

Jamestown colonist John Smith

Jamestown colonist John Smith produced this map of Virginia after his return to England. He marked the villages and lands of the many groups in the Powhatan Confederacy.

Chapter Two

The Trip from England

English Hopes for Its Colony

By the early 1600s, the English had claimed the land north of Florida for themselves. They wanted a new market for their woolen products and a place to send the people from their overcrowded cities. But the government had not been able to build a lasting settlement.

In 1606 King James I signed a **charter** that allowed private companies to start colonies in North America. The companies would provide the money, recruit the settlers, and run the colony as a business. The colony would make money for its company the same way that a farm or a factory might, by producing gold, timber, and agricultural products for sale.

The King's charter gave North America from Pennsylvania to South Carolina to the Virginia Company of London. By the end of the year, the Company had three ships ready to sail—the *Susan Constant*, the *Godspeed*, and the *Discovery*. On board were 140 men, including about 40 sailors, and 4 boys.

The Trip

On December 20, 1606, the three ships set sail. For six weeks they hovered around the English coast, rocked by storms. Many of the men were horribly seasick. Finally the winds shifted and they headed for North America.

After nearly five months at sea, the sailors sighted land in Virginia. After a rough beginning, the sailing had been clear,

The seal of the Virginia Company of London carries a picture of King James I. The seal was used as an official stamp on important papers.

and only one man had died from illness. But there were already quarrels among the men.

Arrival in Virginia

After a few weeks exploring, the settlers found a spot for their colony. Sixty miles (100 kilometers) from the ocean, on a **peninsula** in the river they called the James River after their king, they chose a site on which to build their settlement.

The site, which they named Jamestown Island, had one thing in favor of it: because the strip of land that connected it to the mainland was narrow, the settlers felt it would be easy to defend against attackers. There were some serious problems with the choice, however. The water there was not at all good to drink, and there were a lot of mosquitoes and other insects.

This is a replica of the *Susan Constant*, the biggest of the three ships that took the colonists to Virginia from England.

Great Expectations

"This River which wee have discovered is one of the famousest Rivers that ever was found by any Christian. . . .Wheresoever we landed upon this River, wee saw the goodliest Woods . . . many fruites . . . great plentie of fish of all kindes . . . many great and large Medowes having excellent good pasture for any Cattle. There is also great store of Deere both Red and Fallow. There are Beares, Foxes, Otters, Bevers, Muskats, and wild beasts unknowne."

Colonist George Percy's first impressions of Virginia

Chapter Three

The Struggle to Survive

Idle Hands

"As at this time were most of our chiefest men either sicke or discontented, the rest being in such dispaire, as they would rather starve and rot with idlenes, then be perswaded to do any thing for their owne reliefe."

John Smith

The First Months

The Virginia Company had chosen seven leaders for the colony and sealed their names in a box. Before the settlers went ashore, they opened the box and learned the names of their new leaders. Three were the ships' captains, three were gentlemen, and the last was John Smith, a former army officer. These leaders immediately began to quarrel.

The Virginia Company had directed the settlers to find a fertile place to build their settlement and to begin farming to provide food for the coming winter. The company also ordered the settlers to restock the ships with lumber, **sassafras** root, and metal samples to take back to England at the end of June 1607. By the time the ships sailed, things were already grim in Jamestown. The settlers had done little building or farming. They had suffered one attack by Native people whose land they were taking, and their leaders were still quarreling.

The colonists settled on a peninsula they named Jamestown Island. This view of Jamestown Island today probably looks much as it did to the settlers.

The colonists lived in tents when they first arrived. They set about building houses, but they had no building skills.

Getting Sick

It would get worse. In July, many of the settlers fell ill. Within weeks several were dead of diseases caused by the bad water and the mosquitoes. The supplies the settlers had brought with them were nearly gone, and they had not planted any crops. Nor had they learned how to fish or hunt, and they did not want to leave the settlement because they were afraid of being attacked by Indians. By the end of September, nearly half of the settlers had died.

Those who were left were so sick they could barely bury the dead. The Powhatans could easily have killed them all. Instead, they suddenly arrived in Jamestown one day with lifesaving gifts of food.

John Smith, a Leader Who Worked

At this desperate time, John Smith stepped forward to lead the settlers. Smith had been placed in charge of supplies, and now he put the colonists to work building houses. Never a gentleman himself, he worked alongside them. Although weak and ill, the men were encouraged by his example to start building houses and roof them with **thatch**. Soon, most of the settlers had homes for the winter ahead.

Rescued by the Powhatan

"It pleased God . . . to send those people which were our mortall enemies to releeve us with victuals, as Bread, Corne, Fish, and Flesh in great plentie, which was the setting up of our feeble men, otherwise wee had all perished."

Colonist George Percy

A Visit to Powhatan

With that done, Smith made several trips to trade for food with the Indians, both showing and winning respect. Still, the colonists were careless with their food. Instead of saving for the winter, they ate or wasted all they had.

In December of that first year, Smith and his men made a trip up the Chickahominy River to visit Chief Powhatan. Their boat ran aground in shallow water, but Smith and two other men continued on foot guided by two Native companions.

Other Indians pursued the party of five and killed Smith's men. Then they took Smith captive. After several weeks they brought him before the great Chief Powhatan at his capital of Werowocomoco.

What happened next is the source of the story of John Smith and Pocahontas. John Smith himself told the story. It is very romantic, but it was not the first story he told, and he may have made it up. After all, Smith's first telling of the story does not mention Pocahontas at all, but says that Powhatan sent him home after the two men talked.

John Smith's Story

This is the story John Smith told later. After a great feast, two huge stones were placed in front of Powhatan. Smith's head was laid on them and the Indians got ready to beat his brains out with their clubs. Smith writes in his account, "Pocahontas the King's dearest daughter . . . got his head in her armes, and laid

John Smith wrote in his journal that when he went to visit Powhatan, the chief's daughter Pocahontas saved his life. Nobody knows if this story is true or not.

her owne upon his to save him from death: whereat the Emperour was contented he should live." After that, according to Smith, Powhatan declared them true friends. Smith returned to Jamestown with gifts and good wishes from Powhatan.

New Colonists Arrive

It was January 1608, just seven months since the settlers had arrived from England, when a ship from England arrived in Jamestown. Sent by the Virginia Company, it was loaded with supplies and more than one hundred new colonists. Although they were shocked to find that only thirty-eight of the original colonists were still alive, their hopes were high.

But once again, Jamestown's luck was bad. Just days after the ship arrived, fire swept the settlement, destroying most of the buildings and supplies. This would have meant the end of the settlement, but Powhatan sent food to the starving settlers several times a week, keeping them alive through the winter.

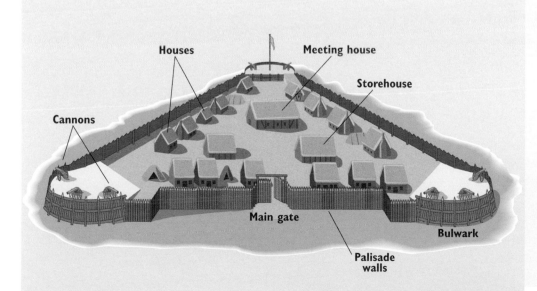

Houses   Meeting house   Storehouse   Cannons   Main gate   Bulwark   Palisade walls

In Jamestown's early days, all the buildings were in a fort enclosed by a triangular **palisade**. In the corners were **bulwarks** from which the fort was defended with cannons.

Gold Rush

The sailors stayed in Jamestown for more than three months, eating the food meant for the settlers and leading them on wild searches for gold. The settlers joined the sailors in loading what they thought was gold onto the ship. When the sailors arrived in England with their cargo of glittering stones, they found out that it was not real gold, but a worthless metal known as fool's gold.

In the spring of 1608, John Smith organized the colonists to repair and rebuild the fort. He also explored the country around the fort and traded with the Indians. In September, the settlers elected Smith president of the colony.

The Winter of 1608–1609

Another boatload of settlers arrived in September, bringing the first women to Jamestown. Throughout the fall, Smith and the colonists rebuilt the fort and stockpiled supplies. That winter found Jamestown in better shape than the one before.

Trading with the Native People

Trade with the Powhatan people was essential to the survival of Jamestown. The Native people of Virginia were as interested in the settlers' metal weapons as the settlers were in obtaining food. In exchange for food and seeds for crops, the colonists also offered woven clothes and blankets, tools, and household items such as iron cooking pots. The Powhatan particularly liked blue glass beads. The one shown here was found at Jamestown and had been made especially for trading.

In the winter of 1609 to 1610, most of the Jamestown settlers died from starvation. This painting shows settlers carrying bodies outside the wall of the fort to be buried.

More colonists arrived in 1609, this time whole families. One ship was lost, but after a terrible trip, four hundred new settlers arrived in Jamestown, sick and weakened. They joined the two hundred colonists already in Jamestown and nearby Indian villages. They settled in two new **outposts** on the James River. But it was late in the year already, too late to plant for the winter.

The Starving Time

At the end of 1609, a gunpowder accident sent John Smith back to England. Without Smith to organize their work and trade with the Indians, the settlers saw things get steadily worse throughout the winter that became known as the Starving Time. They soon ran out of grain with over six hundred people to feed. The Indians stopped trading with them and killed their pigs. Fearing attack, the colonists were afraid to leave the fort to hunt or fish. By spring only sixty people were still alive. Some colonists died from cold, illness, and Indian attacks, but most of them starved to death.

Rescue

The few remaining colonists were about to give up when help arrived in the form of Lord De La Warr. King James had decided that the colonists could not run their own affairs and appointed Lord De La Warr as a governor. Governor De La Warr arrived with three hundred healthy colonists and enough supplies for one year.

Trying Again

The new government made several changes in how Jamestown was being run. Each man had a specific job: planting crops, making bricks, or building houses. The settlers dug toilets and a new well. Those who didn't or couldn't work were denied food.

The governor also allowed free, male colonists to rent land and keep what they grew. Each free man received 3 acres (1.2 hectares) to farm for himself. Now that everything they raised did not have to go back to the Virginia Company, the men were willing to work harder. By 1619, the new government allowed colonists to own their own land, but

As the colony grew, the settlers moved out beyond the fort. This painting shows how the settlement may have looked in 1614.

18

The wedding of Pocahontas, or Rebecca, to John Rolfe in April 1614. John Rolfe was the settler who introduced tobacco to Jamestown.

it also enforced rules of behavior. Crimes included sewing shirts of the wrong length, speaking against the Virginia Company, and running off to live in Native villages. Those who broke the rules could be whipped, or executed.

The colonists started to raise tobacco and sent four barrels back to England, where it sold well. Soon tobacco became the first source of income for the new colony.

Troubles with Indians

After John Smith left, the Indians and colonists did not get along well at all. Trade had stopped, and the settlers stole corn from Native fields and storehouses. They had also been taking more and more Powhatan land. The Indians in return had taken captives.

In 1613, the colonists took captive Powhatan's daughter, Pocahontas. They held her hostage until 1614, when she married John Rolfe, one of the settlers. The marriage brought peace between the settlers and the Indians. But when John Rolfe took his new wife, now named Rebecca, on a visit to England, she became sick and died there in 1617.

Chapter Five

Life in Virginia

Life in Virginia

In 1616, there were about 350 people living in Virginia in four settlements. Only about 50 of them lived in Jamestown. By 1624, more than 7,300 people had come to Virginia, but more than 6,000 of them had died. People were realizing that only pigs and cattle did well on Jamestown Island. They began to move into the surrounding countryside, where the land and water were better.

Tobacco

Smoking tobacco had become very popular in England and other European countries. Two years after the first barrels of

The House of Burgesses

In 1619, the Virginia Company of London decided it needed to make Virginia a more agreeable place for colonists to live. It gave settlers more land of their own and got rid of some of the strict laws. The company also set up a new local government called the House of **Burgesses**. This was a group made up of leaders, or burgesses, from each district of Virginia. The House of Burgesses

made laws and dealt with local issues. The trouble was the burgesses were the richest men and biggest landowners—there were no women or servants. So they made laws that were mostly for their own benefit.

20

tobacco made their way to the English market, the Virginia colony was sending 50,000 pounds (23,000 kilograms) a year. It had become the colony's **cash crop**, and settlers used it instead of money.

Tobacco farming required many workers, and so landowners paid for indentured servants to come and work for seven years. The servants were kept in terrible conditions, with poor housing and little food. After seven years, they were supposed to be given tools and seed to start their own farms, but most of them died before they were free.

Here Come the Brides

The Virginia Company knew that its colony had to have women if it was going to attract and keep single men there. So in 1620 and 1621, the company sent nearly 250 women to Virginia to become brides. The men paid at least 120 pounds (55 kg) of tobacco for a wife.

A Loathsome Custom

"[Smoking is] a custome lothsome to the eye, hatefull to the Nose, harmefull to the braine, daungerous to the Lungs, and in the blacke stinking fume thereof, neerest to resembling the horrible Stigian smoke of the pit that is bottomelesse."

King James I of England

The first brides arrive in Jamestown from England. Although they were advertised as "young maidens," many of them were convicts, shipped overseas instead of being sent to prison.

21

Tobacco barrels are loaded onto ships in James River. In 1628, more than 500,000 pounds (230,000 kg) of tobacco were shipped from Jamestown.

Families and Farming

Most of Virginia's settlers were now families. They were farmers and planters whose dream was to live like rich Englishmen. They wanted land, money, and an easy life where someone else did the work. In England this would not have been possible because a few families already owned all the land, but in Virginia, accumulating land was easy.

In 1619, the head of a household was awarded 50 acres (20 ha) of land for each person he brought to Virginia. This meant that men who had slaves and indentured servants could grab up hundreds of acres of land for themselves.

Indian Wars

When Chief Powhatan died in 1618, the peace of Pocahontas was broken. The settlers continued to seize Indian land for their tobacco crops and their growing settlements. The Native people were losing their homes and their cornfields.

In 1622, an Indian attack on Henrico, one of the settlements in Virginia, resulted in the capture or deaths of 350 of the 1,400 settlers and destroyed the town. The attacks continued by both sides, but by 1700 only 1,000 remained of the once-powerful Powhatan people. The white settlers had claimed their homeland.

Plantation Society

By the mid-1600s, there were hundreds of farms in Virginia connected to the settlements by a network of roads. But Jamestown itself did not flourish and became little more than a town to pass through on the way to the tobacco **plantations**. The earlier settlers in Jamestown had planned to grab the land's riches and take them back to England. But the new planters of Virginia were here to stay, to form a **ruling class**.

Powhatan was succeeded as chief of the Powhatan by Opechan-canough, his brother (shown above, with his warriors). To try and save the Powhatan from being forced out of Virginia, Ope-chancanough attacked the Virginia colony. In 1644, he was finally captured and killed.

Slavery In Virginia

In 1619 a Dutch ship had arrived in Jamestown with twenty Africans to sell to the colonists as slaves. But the colonists had their indentured servants and didn't need many slaves right then. By 1670, however, fewer servants were coming willingly from England, and the market was better for the slave traders. Virginia later passed a law that said that all servants who came by sea and were not Christians were slaves. By 1681, there were 3,000 slaves in Virginia, a number that grew to 260,000 by 1782.

Chapter Six

The End of Jamestown

This tobacco label from the early 1700s shows a rich plantation owner overseeing his slaves.

A Cash Crop

Virginia now had a cash crop that it could sell anywhere, and it began trading with more countries. In order to keep control, England passed a law saying that only English ships could carry goods to and from the colonies. The Virginians did not want to give up their trade with the Dutch, however, and continued to do business with them.

The Colonists Protest

The English also imposed high taxes on tobacco. It was hard for many to make a living selling their crop when prices were low. The colonists began to protest about taxes and other issues. As the colony grew, settlers were taking more land, and the Indians were fighting back. All these difficult problems led to a revolt that became known as Bacon's Rebellion.

Bacon's Rebellion

Nathaniel Bacon was a landowner who had settled on the outskirts of the Virginia colony. He wanted permission from the colony to fight against Indians to secure his land. But the colony's leaders had trade agreements with the Native groups and were trying to keep peace with them. Bacon and his supporters led an army of five hundred men into Jamestown in June 1676. They demanded support for a war against the Indians. When they met with the governor and his council, the rebels also proposed **reforms** in the way the colony was run. These were passed by the colony and became known as Bacon's Laws.

Bacon, however, was soon denounced as a traitor for stirring up trouble. In September 1676, he marched into Jamestown once again. This time the governor fled, and Bacon and his men burned the town to the ground. But when Bacon died of illness in October of that same year, the rebellion collapsed.

In spite of the agreements between the Virginia colony and the Native people around it, white settlers were taking more and more Indian land. Here, Virginia colonists attack a Native settlement in 1675.

The End of the Jamestown Settlement

Jamestown never really recovered after all its disasters and setbacks, but it remained Virginia's capital until 1698. In that year, a fire burned down the statehouse and the government of the colony was moved to nearby Williamsburg. By 1700, Jamestown was abandoned and the island became part of two local plantations.

Conclusion

Dressed in colonial clothes, people at the recreated Jamestown fort show visitors what life was like in the early days of the settlement.

Rediscovering Jamestown

For many years, people thought the land on which the original Jamestown fort stood had been washed out to sea. In 1996, however, **archaeologists** discovered remains of the fort. Since then, they have found other parts of the fort, including three storage cellars and a pit filled with armor and weapons. Altogether, archaeologists have found more than 350,000 items from the earliest days of Jamestown.

Jamestown Today

Today, near to where Jamestown once stood, visitors can see the remains of two cultures that—for a time—shared the land and their lives. Jamestown Settlement is a living museum where people can see how colonists and Native people lived.

The Powhatan village at Jamestown Settlement offers demonstrations of Native American crafts, such as the tanning of deerskins shown here.

At a reconstructed Powhatan village, visitors can watch Native people weave, grind corn, and make ropes and canoes.

The recreated fort shows how Jamestown may have looked in about 1610. There are even replicas of the three ships that traveled to Virginia in 1607.

Learning from Artifacts

The **artifacts** the archaeologists have found teach much about how the Powhatans and Jamestown settlers lived together. Glass beads and copper necklaces survive, showing what the English traded for food from the Indians. The styles of clay pots and pipes help date other material found with them in the pits. The large number of broad ax heads, used for chopping trees and shaping the lumber, shows that wood was a necessity in Jamestown. It was used for heat, for building, for cooking, and for trade.

These two artifacts from early Jamestown are (*left*) a funnel from a food mill and (*right*) the head of an axe.

1606	April 10: King James I of England grants the Virginia Company of London the right to start a colony in North America. December 20: Three ships set sail for Virginia from London, England.
1607	May 14: Colonists land at Jamestown Island and found the settlement of Jamestown. July: Colonists start to get sick and die. December: According to legend, Pocahontas saves John Smith's life.
1608	September: Smith is elected president of Virginia colony. First female colonists arrive in Jamestown.
1609	King James I appoints governor for Virginia colony. October: John Smith returns to England. Starving Time begins.
1610	June: Governor De La Warr arrives as colonists prepare to abandon Jamestown.
1613	Pocahontas is taken hostage.
1614	Pocahontas marries John Rolfe. First shipment of tobacco is sent from Jamestown to England.
1617	Pocahontas dies.
1618	Powhatan dies and Opechancanough becomes leader of the Powhatan Confederacy.
1619	House of Burgesses is founded. Colonists are given land grants.
1622	March: Powhatan people capture or kill 350 Virginia colonists.
1676	Bacon's Rebellion.
1698	October: Statehouse in Jamestown burns down.
1699	Capital of Virginia is moved to Williamsburg.

Things to Think About and Do

Arriving in Jamestown

It is 1609 and you are ten years old. You have always lived in the big, busy city of London, and you have never left England before. Now you have traveled to Virginia on a ship as one of the first families to go to the colony. Describe your impressions and feelings when you arrive at Jamestown. What are the people like? How does your family set about making a home and getting food?

Fortified Villages

Look at the Algonquian village in the picture on page 6. Now look at the picture of the early fort at Jamestown on page 15. What is the same? What is different?

Struggle to Survive

Why do you think the people in Jamestown had such a struggle to survive? What do you think they could have done differently?

Running Away

A number of Jamestown colonists ran away from their own settlement when things got bad and went to live with the Powhatan people. Imagine that you are one of those colonists. Compare your new life to your life in Jamestown.

Glossary

archaeologist: person who studies remains of earlier human cultures.

artifact: something made by humans remaining from an earlier time.

bulwark: Wall or other structure that acts as a defense against attack.

burgess: male, white landowner who represented his district of Virginia in the House of Burgesses.

cash crop: crop, such as tobacco or coffee, grown mainly to sell rather than to provide food for the farmer.

charter: official grant from a government or ruler.

colony: settlement, area, or country owned or controlled by another nation.

confederacy: alliance of groups that agree to act together and support each other.

fortify: make stronger.

indentured servant: worker who agrees to work for a set period of time in exchange for an opportunity offered by an employer.

New World: name for North and South America used by the first Europeans who traveled and settled there. They thought of themselves as from the "Old World" (Europe).

outpost: small settlement that is a distant part of a bigger settlement.

palisade: fence made of sharp wooden stakes.

peninsula: piece of land jutting out into water but connected to mainland.

plantation: large farm growing cash crops where work is done by laborers or slaves.

reform: change made to improve social conditions for people.

ruling class: group of people that holds the power in a community.

sassafras: tree, of which the root is used as a flavoring for drinks.

swampy: very wet. Used to describe land sometimes partly under water.

thatch: dried grasses tightly woven and used for roofing material.

Further Information

Books

Bulla, Clyde Robert. *Pocahontas and the Strangers*. Scholastic, 1995.

Graves, Charles P. *John Smith*. Chelsea House, 1991.

Knight, James E. *Jamestown: New World Adventure* (*Adventures in Colonial America*). Troll, 1998.

Sakurai, Gail. *The Jamestown Colony*. Children's Press, 1997.

Sita, Lisa. *Indians of the Northeast: Traditions, History, Legends, and Life*. Gareth Stevens, 2001.

Web Sites

www.apva.org Pictures from the Association for the Preservation of Virginia Antiquities of archaeological explorations and artifacts found at Jamestown.

www.historyisfun.org Information about Jamestown Settlement from the Jamestown-Yorktown Foundation.

www.vcdh.virginia.edu/jamestown The University of Virginia's Virtual Jamestown project.

Useful Addresses

Jamestown Settlement
Jamestown-Yorktown Foundation
P. O. Box 1607
Williamsburg, VA 23187.
Telephone: 1-888-593-4682

Index

Page numbers in **bold** indicate pictures.

Algonquians, 4, **4**, 6–8, **6**, **7**, **8**, 9
    houses and villages, 6, **6**, 7, **8**, 9,
    17, **25**

Bacon, Nathaniel, 25
Bacon's Rebellion, 25

colonies, 4, 10
colonists, 18, 22
    conflict among, 11, 12
    death of, 11, 13, 14, 15, 17, **17**, 20,
    21, 23
    families, 17, 22
    first arrival in Virginia, 4, 9, 11
    identity of, 4
    later arrivals, 15, 16, 17, 18, 20,
    21, **21**
    women, 16, 20, 21, **21**

De La Warr, Thomas, 18

England, 4, 5, **5**, 10, 15, 16, 19, 22,
    23, 24

farmers and farming, 4, 5, 7, **8**, 12, 16,
    18, 21, 22
fishing, 7, **7**, 13, 17
food and supplies, 7, 8, 12, 13, 15, 16,
    17, 18, 19

gold, 5, 16

Henrico, 23
House of Burgesses, 20, **20**,
hunting, 7, 13, 17

indentured servants, 5, 20, 21, 22, 23

James I, King, 10, 11, **10**, 18, 21
Jamestown, **15**, **18**, 20, 23
    attacks on, 12, 13, 17, 19, 23, 25

Jamestown *continued*
    building of, 12, 13, **13**, 16, 18, 27
    discoveries at, **16**, 26, 27, **27**
    end of, 24–25
    founding of, 4, 9, 11, 12
    housing in, 13, **13**, 15, 18
    site of, 11, **12**
Jamestown Settlement, 26–27, **26**, **27**

land grants, 10, 18, 22

Opechancanough, 23, **23**
outposts, 17

plantations, 23, 24, 25
Pocahontas, 14–15, **14**, 19, **19**, 22
Powhatan, Chief, 9, 14, **14**, 15, 19,
    22, 23
Powhatan people, 9, 13, 14, 16, 17, 19,
    23, **23**, 27, **27**,
    land, 9, **9**, 12, 19, 22–23, 25

Rolfe, John, 19, **19**

settlers, *see* colonists
sickness and disease, 10, 12, 13, 15, 17
slavery and slaves, 5, 22, 23, **24**,
Smith, John, 7, 9, 12, 14, **14**, 15, 16,
    17, 19
starvation, 4, 15, 17
Starving Time, 17, **17**

taxes, 24
tobacco, 19, 20–21, , 22, **22**, 23, 24
trade, 14, 16, 17, 19, 24, 25, 27

Virginia, 4, **5**, 9, **9**, 20–23, 24, 25
    before white settlement, 6–7, 9
    growth of colony, 10, 17, 18, 20, 25
Virginia Company of London, 10, 12,
    15, 18, 19, 20, 21

Williamsburg, 25